BROKEN LIKE JOB

April 28, 2013

For Mitko

With great affection and respect for your luminous spirit —

Love,
Dimi

BROKEN LIKE JOB

DONNA DENIZÉ

THE WORD WORKS
CAPITAL COLLECTION
WASHINGTON, D.C.

BROKEN LIKE JOB
Copyright © 2005 by Donna Denizé

Reproduction of any part of this book in any form or
by any means, electronic or mechanical, including
photocopying, must be with permission in writing from
the publisher. Address inquiries to:

The WORD WORKS
PO Box 42164
Washington, DC 20015
editor@wordworksdc.com

Cover art by Theodore Moore

Book design, typography by Janice Olson

Library of Congress Number: 2004117199
International Standard Book Number: 0-915380-60-9

Acknowledgements

I am very grateful to my colleagues at St. Albans, especially those who generously offered a gallon-measure of time and faith in these words: Classics teacher, scholar, and friend Wallace Ragan; Shauna Seliy, Writer in Residence (2003-04); Alison Kornet, English teacher and colleague; Norman Constantine, computer teacher and friend who gave technical assistance and encouragement; Rick Peabody, who always answered my calls with kindness; Karren Alenier and Hilary Tham, my editors, whose belief in me and this book gave my spirit sustenance from the table.

I wish to thank the following publishers for historical information and excerpts which appear in some poems: Orbis Books, *In the Parish of the Poor, Writings from Haiti* by Jean-Bertrand Aristide (1990); University Press of America, *Written in Blood, The Story of the Haitian People, 1492-1995* by Michael Heinl (1996); and from *The Odyssey* by Homer, translated by Robert Fagles copyright (c) 1996 by Robert Fagles. Published by Viking Penguin, a division of Penguin Group (USA) Inc.

Grateful acknowledgement is also made to the editors of the following anthologies and magazines in which versions of these poems appeared or will appear: *Whose Woods These Are*, "Noonsigns"; *Provincetown Arts*, "Mengele"; *WPFW Poetry Anthology*, "Luna"; *World Order*, "Toward the Silence"; *Gargoyle #39/40*, "Running the Big River"; *Hungry As We Are*, "Alzheimer's"; *Weavings 2000, The Maryland Millennial Anthology*, "Primer"; *Gargoyle #49*, "Reconsidering Job," "Sacred Geometry," and "Babylon to Baghdad."

To Aunt Jeanne Moore whose courage
and conviction to make a better world
continue the spiritual struggle
our ancestors began, and to my mother,
Emily Irene Elliott, who was both
a poet and poem.

"So powerful is the light of unity that it
can illuminate the whole earth."

BAHA'U'LLAH

Contents

Reconsidering Job	11
Alzheimer's	13
Configurations	14
Babylon to Baghdad	19
Bards Still Sing	21
Not Summons Nor Reckoning	22
Mummy Alice	24
Jewel of the Caribbean	27
Crepusculo	45
Job's Wife Speaks	49
Mengele	52
Seedling Remembrance	54
Pangaea	55

Noonsigns	59
Song	62
To the Aquarium, Brighton Beach	63
Primer	64

Luna	66
Gathering	67
Climbing	68
Birth	69
Seed the Unbroken Land	70

The Man from Virginia	73
Odysseus in the Underworld	81
Toward the Silence	83
Running the Big River	86
Map Reading	90
Worlds From Babel, Two Towers, 9/11	92
A Sacred Geometry	93
Florence	95
Petrarch	96
Boccaccio	97
Dying for Religion	98
For Love	99
Satori	100
Home (Cape Cod)	102

Endnotes	*107*
About the Author	*115*
About the Capital Collection	*116*
About the Word Works	*117*

Reconsidering Job

> *But put forth thy Hand now, and touch all that he has, and he will curse thee to thy Face.* JOB, 1: 11-12
> *... put forth thy Hand now, and touch his bone and flesh, and he will curse thee.* JOB, 2: 5

What can break to pieces the shameless winters,
these suffering seasons passing through
a habit of heart, minds eternalized

frozen in sorrow where thought splinters, cracks,
breaks in looking for cause? Whether against
a nation or only a man like Job

who lost all, Job looking beyond words,
or conversation which did not include him,
the open mouth, covered and cut off, cries,

drops. Days—pouring once from prosperous
stores—are hours with no answer or light.
For mercy, O Job stood still, considering

"snow's still treasures, proud waves and morning star,
hail, peacock's wing, cedars and shady trees,"
so say *we* endure humiliations:

lost issue, love's disdain, false friends or
ulcerous eruptions that can not bring
rest to our beds, not a moment's

peace from nations where we hear the talkers
talking and know the dark of starless nights.
But which of *us* is like Job, "who drinketh up

scorning like water," suffering afflictions
come on unknown winds, bearing beauty, once
more, blessings from unseen deserts, and

bearing toil, where substance or sickness grows
as a whirlwind in the Spirit of His
breath against nations or only a man.

Alzheimer's

Could I give you an anchor, I would. Weight,
something to hold you in a place that digs
to bottom of past, floor of memory,

but all is sinking, as I grasp for the
ring, stock, shank of your life—something to slip
a knot through, to tie you to ancestors.

For in this place that is neither here nor
there, you are forsaken by days, days that
were your own, and years honored in pictures

and emblems of love are wind passing through
an old woman's thin grey hair till all is
life we cannot hold from time's undertow.

Still, love is not estrangement, and I will
seek you, seek you there in the eye of it,
the face of earth, stars, for one moment more.

Configurations

Aeidei di 'Emou Pham Thic Trin,
Aeidei di 'Emou.

All things are full of gods,
philosophers say, but what is to keep

us from forgetting history as an old
love letter, memory and loss inventing

the reading, and the remembrance
of things, a fiction sent from those who

remember the earth full of goddesses
and gods?
    Or what to prevent us feeling
each generation as a burden to

the next, till old Adam bends young backs
and what one knows is lost, useless, or in

need of a crutch for life's urgency fosters
forgetting, and it is miracle we remember

remember to speak at all…

I. Montagnard Soldier: "Did you Hear?"

"Son My? It was thirteen years before
death chose a day to fall on their houses.
I was a boy watching his father with other

mountain men returning from hills in evening.
Each day fighting with homemade weapons, guns
taken from the dead. From them, I learned

to fight the dying that surrounded us. Of
Son My I have little memory, but
the old woman can tell you how a child

came out of Son My moving across fields,
like a miracle. The girl lives still
in the family house, tending the land

and the monument. I only remember
voices carried the news like waves
from the old woman's hut: 'Did you hear,

did you hear how Pham Thic Trin is living?'
'Where?' 'In the house of the old blind Van Duc.'
'What saved her?'"
      Some say
   it was the ghosts of the others, some say
   it was a goddess or god.

II. *Jewel Van Duc:* "Sing through Me"

"At first, she did not speak and no one noticed
her, till she walked up to me, Jewel Van Duc,
and tugged this old woman on the elbow.

So I, Van Duc, named her *Girl Bodhisattva,*
and told the child with no village or family,
Do not despair, they are here singing

through you. Remember when your father
would say, 'This little village has no luck'?
Well, you live, you live, now no one will forget.

We called it Son My, but the soldiers called
it My Lai. My Lai one, two, three, four, five.
My Lai, till all of Southeast Asia was

death's little village. I am one old voice
among them, like one mountain among many,
but she, she is the miracle of Son My,

village where no one walks. You see, she came
from the burning, the ditch, while everyone
was looking the other way, and I was

there when she would dream the dream, I was there
to ask, 'Pham, is it the nightmare again?'
Even when asleep, the heart is awake.

'Wake, tell your dream, and I will listen
as you tell me, tell me again what you see.'"

    Moving over field, trees rising to meet
    a message of air, longing to dream leaves
    fall from trees, light leaving the mountains,

    auntie and mother sowing, as village
    voices fade into North, East, South, West
    to rest where grandmother's graying hair does

    not turn to stone. During the day, you go
    go to the monument, during the night
    to a ditch spilling shades, seeking blood.

III. *Ephialtes Niht maere Pesadilla Cauchmar Nightmare Cơn ác mông:*

    dreams bodies still as dolls, dreams
    borders, sleep lifts you trembling, swept aside
    fluttering out of you, shaking dolls
    dragged into fields, limbs
    unfeeling, air does not rise, falling down
    does not rise what did not
    perish *perish* in you, something

above you, everywhere lifeless things: floor,
spinning wheel, cup, glove,
worlds, *weeping,* smiling
empty rooms, dream *dream*
sun drops light over Southeast Asia
green life, night, bamboo (and who
sings to the plucking string?) cannot forget
go *go* from ditch, twenty years, *silence brings father's
voice,* always his voice in wind calling
a village, *house, bucket, pot, ghost
circling rooms:* mother washing, child, soap
water spilling, laugh, sing auntie sing stitch stitch
stitch walls to house no longer house
village bound, no air just waking waking
waking and wind calling, *Get up, Get up!*

'"Pham, can you hear me? It is Jewel Van Duc.
Wake and tell me of the last face you saw;
I will listen till the burning becomes

horizon, till the cool breeze blows across
our backs and the sun drops warmth upon
the living, gathering cassava, corn, rice.'

You see, I am there when she dreams; I am
there when she wakes. And it was ten years
before she journeyed back to Son My to live

in that house. Ten years, I tell you, she is nineteen
and I, eighty. I begged her not to leave
living for the dead, but she could not hear

me, and now she lives in that house, during
the day she goes to the monument,
during the night she goes to the ditch;

she could not hear me, but I understand,
monuments are for the living. The dead,
the dead need no reminders."

IV. *Pham Thic Trin, Son My sings through you...*

    My Lai Aeidei dia Sou.

Buddha, bamboo, this pot, blanket, wood, house,
fire: "All things are full of gods," and each

day you seek them, walking into history.
In each night journey, you join a grandfather,

a village, images in the blood, unrestrained
as wind.

Babylon to Baghdad

One way to remember: sovereign palace, sacred
precinct, ziggurat, or hanging gardens
resembling mountains, Persian mountains,
clouds floating over inner and outer walls, and

bricks lining a Fertile Crescent—the work of gods!
Where Marduk wrapped in destiny's
tablets and large, circular human eyes
strained to see the Divine; or priests,

revealers of word in cuneiform, pictograms,
records of life between two rivers, land's sweet
savors, morning breeze, and moat awash in
splendors of sun. Who speaks now of

the place and ancient river bed, of a city
consumed each time it flooded, or life
by the Euphrates' flow, inevitable
moving, moving west beyond them,

beyond brick—pile of brick left on the plain
of story retold in tablets, flood, or
one priest, man, climbing mountain of the Divine—
a spirit, river flowing through the land,

land of toppled temples, once sacred precincts.
His memory, sacred words like rivers
borne on human shoulders moving moving,
river of ache and heart lament:

*Would that I had died before this, and
been forgotten, forgotten!* Grief wide

as rivers flowing, through lands, through Prophets
bearing a staff and words to kings. Laws led

from Babylon to Ur, Jerusalem
to Mecca—cities of revelation,
scripture and tablets, memories multiplied
melted to idols, curses, consternation

of soul, till only remnant remembers
scepters, river gods, prophet, staff, ancient
Law on tablets; and woe, light forgotten,
forsaken bricks on plains of ruin:

heat and bombs of Baghdad, Babylon—
Armageddon. Ziggurat. Eden.

Embattled empires enter once more
this land, weary and wet with tears; *Would that I
had died before this, and been forgotten, forgotten,*
or that *we* who be might see its green, a Gate

of God, river flow in the Fertile Crescent
of heart's fortified city, eyes open
to Voice, to hearts over clouds, riverbeds
wall-worn cities, glittering gods, worlds, worlds

wrapped once more in the raiment of Light.

Bards Still Sing

Beneath tattered rags a bard still plays
to sing morning's rising in tenderly lays,
but if only for beauty the gods did sing,
then what of this age and its terrible ring?
When flutes are grown silent, the harp out of tune,
and the weak or the violent fill the house—every room.

Not Summons Nor Reckoning

He did not recover from one wound before
another report followed hard, fast,

came to him as words rushing in a whirlwind
of trouble, whirlpool of grief. Stunned and dazed

he fell to his knees, he fell to his knees
wanting, praying, awaiting reply.

He would have even preferred being
summoned, summoned to a reckoning

for misery with motive would not sadden,
or bring him such remorse. And so it was

and came to be that what he wanted most
in answer to his own was Voice, heard above

winds, above clouds of mystery from those
whose words bore storms to his heart, floods

in a heart uttering words like dust. Yes,
Job wanted something, not visible company,

but something to reach, reach to and be heard
or held. So say: we are broken, broken like

Job, wanting a flood of grace filling the
palm of hand, cup, or gallon-measure, filling

water, clay, desire and every thing
from dust created: East Bank, West Bank

Israel   Jerusalem   Palestine
Columbine—tumbling towers—Iraq and

Baghdad falling. Snipers, spies, Patriot
Act, Haiti rebel cause Haiti—presence,

visitation, to seize revolutions,
destiny's wheel and spheres of life caught

in the whirlpool—whether spent force or complete
cohesion—like passions contending.

Oh to be heard, held by mercy, held from
forces bent on reducing it—us—to

utter impotence, heart-fire, and this:
a world worn by gathering storms. So Job

wanted something, the Mighty Arm, its work,
works from Job to his cradle: rumblings, light's

splendors, unfailing blessing and every
thing from worlds of dust proclaiming Presence.

The majesty, simplicity of it
cracks the heart, it cracks the heart open.

Mummy Alice

    Jean-Robert discovered diplomacy,
(they say) when car and driver pulled up,
and she asked would he like a ride, a ride
in her new car, "Oh yes, Mummy Alice!"
as he glided into the back beside her.
And wonder filled his eyes, but hers, poised
straight-ahead, never moving, except
to motion a driver, placid as stone,
to **Go**. And car moved over gravel, rocks
and dirt, and they sat in stone silence

for an hour of eternity. Soon, his longing—
only to end silence, "Mummy Alice,
you don't have a radio, if you had a radio
in your car, you could listen to music."
She didn't answer, never even moved
her head. Perhaps, *perhaps*, she'd not heard,
so his gaze turned to window, land and sky,
to people passing momentary as pictures
by his face, hot, wet, as he tried to lower
his window, a glass letting cool air pass

over skin sweating from August sun;
but it was as motionless as mountains,
as Haiti, and inscrutable as Mummy Alice.
And boy-excitement grew, grew as seedlings
seeking water, grew as unquenchable desire
rose to sound, "Mummy Alice, your car
should have electric windows." Nothing.
Had she heard? He turned his shoulders
to her rigid profile to breathe syllables rising like heat,

"Haiti is hot, yes?" **Yes**. "And you are rich, yes?"
Yes. "Then your car could have air
conditioning, and then you'd could stay cool,
and people would know you're rich!" His body
stiffened like one dead as she told the driver
Stop the car, and turned at last, to face
his words with her words **Get out.**
"What?" **Get out!** Cut to his core, he
could utter only "But, we're far from
home; I don't know where we are
Or how to get back." And he

could not, dared not speak more, remembered
only watching in silence that sliced like
a knife, as car slid away in trails
of dust. Frightened, frozen, he, a boy
of five sat by the road and cried an hour,
an hour, before she glided slowly
alongside him, stopped, doors locked,
and faced him. Down down her window
rolled, **Do you like my car now?**
as he wiped his tears—tears she hated—

and gave his offering, "Oh yes, Mummy Alice,
I like your car very much!" and her words
only **Get in.** This, all he heard as he slid, chastened,
once more into the back beside her,
and she nodded to the driver **Go**.

That's how her grandson, a boy of five or six
(they tell me), learned she was hard, hard
as nails, felt her iron, shrewd silence,

silence immovable as the only image I own,
the only photograph I've seen of her:
at Aunt Gladys's wedding—Mummy Alice

smiling, statuesque, striding down
an aisle, hair pulled tightly back
into a bun, a buxom woman in her fifties,

finely dressed. Only met her once
at eighty, a woman, hunched over, stripped
of body, hair loosely fallen about her face,

wrinkled, withered, wracked by illness
and skin she feared to shed; driven, she moved
from hospital to hospital, doctor to doctor:

Paris, Canada, New York till she told
them all, **No more cutting!** Confident
stride gone now, she shuffled from room

to room like a frightened bird.

Jewel of the Caribbean

I.
And to the land's accuser the Lord said:

"Have you considered My island? No place
on earth so fruitful, blessed by coconut,
cassava, coffee; not even robbers

murderers, or personal desires
given full rein, not striving to improve
its condition while the motive is one's

own gain, no, not whirlwinds ruin My land's
sharp turning." Tale from land of the mountains,
Haiti, where missionaries brought bibles

and leaders came, but from a distance, they
saw the suffering was great. And now, they
did not recognize a land greatly changed.

> When Job's three friends, Eliphaz of Teman, Bildad
> of Shuah, and Zophar of Naamah, heard of all these
> calamities... they left their homes and arranged to come
> and condole with him... comfort him. But when they first
> saw him from a distance, they did not recognize him... For
> seven days and seven nights, they sat beside him on the
> ground, and none of them said a word to him; for they
> saw that his suffering was very great.
> JOB, 2: 11-13

And believing we knew what had made him so blue
we guests, uninvited, (well-meaning, it's true!),
sat down to deep silence to watch as days waned,
but wrapped our hearts firmly away from his pain,
our hope to bring comfort to him we once knew.
To come and condole in lands where Death slew.

II.

In the beginning, Hayti, like Job. Haiti,
so many trying to lead from afar.
Man and land so altered and changed that from
a distance, they did not recognize him:

Macandal   Oge and   Chavannes: led slave
    insurrection, took arms against French.
Toussaint L' Ouverture invaded, marched, declared
    slavery abolished.

Dessalines declared Haitian Independence, was
    betrayed and killed.
Petion declared president for life, soon died.

Christophe crowned King Henry I of Haiti, later took
    his own life.
Boyer elected president for life, abdicated, sailed for
    Jamaica.
Oppression, dream, insurrection, disaster,
and travail begat Haiti's Presidents:

Riviere-Herard   Guerrier   Pierrot

Soulouque   Geffard   Salnave   Nissage-Saget

Domingue   Boisrond-Canal   Salomon

Legitime   Hippolyte   Simon Sam

Nord Alexis   Antoine Simon   Auguste

Oreste   Zamor   Theodore   Guillaume Sam

And believing they wept for those whose lives
were hard, presidents came to know wreckage,
one human agony of multitudes; and
came to know dismay, distrust—to know

> Man learns his lesson on a bed of pain. (33: 19)

1915: TO KEEP   KEEP ORDER   U.S. MARINES IN
      P**ORT-AU-P**RINCE,
A**MERICANS   TOOK CHARGE** H**AITIAN CUSTOM HOUSES**
      TOOK CHARGE

Three more presidents: Borno   Roy   Vincent.
E**NDS** A**MERICAN OCCUPATION**   ENDS?
    and another: Lescot
1941: DECLARED   H**AITI DECLARED WAR ON ALL** A**XIS**
      POWERS.

They, too, dreamt a President's dream: Estime
    Magloire   Pierre-Louis
    (Sylvain   Fignole: ephemeral presidencies)

Ephemeral prosperity, enduring trials,
so each one came to condole and comfort
a land whose suffering was very great.
Like those before them, all spoke words,
words which came, once more, from whirling
hearts that said they felt God, knew His justice.

III.
1957: Francois Duvalier elected President

Schooled for a time in the U.S.,
Papa Doc had a look. He seemed intellectual—
his glasses, charming smile, the simple, austere
habits of a doctor—Minister of Labor
and Public Health—a President hoping
to free Haiti from colonialist past,
from puppetry of nations, testing democracy
and suffering soil. Civilian, favored
in Washington to bring progress to Haiti.
And as he came to his position, came
to position his place as Haiti's
President, everything changed; schooled in vagaries

of Haitian past—Toussaint, Christophe, Dessalines—
his ancestors, and griots alive—
Duvalier had changed. They said, he always
carried a tattered copy of *The Prince*
in his pocket, and his glacial eyes—unblinking.

1959: U.S. sends aid to Haiti,

and Washington said, "Duvalier—the man to cure
 Haiti's ills, a man worthy of support."

1959: Duvalier: "I have mastered the country. I have
 mastered power. I am the New Haiti. ...No earthly
 power can prevent me from accomplishing my
 historic mission because it is God and Destiny
 who have chosen me. ...Never forget that I am the

supreme authority of the State. Henceforth, I, I
alone, I am your only master."

But even robbers,
murderers, whirlwinds
ranging over earth
could not rob people
of their dream.

When Duvalier spoke of Communism—
Communists in the Caribbean,
to keep, keep Washington off balance:

**1960-61: U.S. GRANTED
GIFTS TO HAITI: $40 MILLION**
and Duvalier accepted, refused U.S. advice

for roads, equipment, airport. In Haiti
Duvalier dealings. Duvalier,
dealing with U.S.—shrewd, politician.

Not even
    robbers
        marauders

            whirlwinds

ranging over earth could rob the blameless
of dreams, a people, blameless and upright.

Yes, at crossroads and sacred thresholds, their
tom-toms, horns, and calypso would roll death
away, roll death away from each door, house,
village and town in dance—carnivals—song.

No, even invaders and murderers,
whose whirlwinds reared palaces for themselves,
delivered them to the conqueror's hands,
sighs and tears, did not cause them to curse You.

1962-64: Not Duvalier dealings, dealing
to Haiti, Republic of Haiti: his attacks,
assaults against students, priests, bishops,
as Tonton Macoutes took them to prison,
and bombs exploded, and schools—surrounded
and universities—by police; Haitian
vagrancies entangled with vagaries
U.S. make their feet leave the earth like
a river: flood, waves let loose, scorched earth...
executions   hostages   jailings
beatings   arrests   peasants crucified
relatives   swept up   never seen again
guerrilla campaign   heads chopped off,
delivered to Duvalier on president's
orders. Purges—Duvalier, Vatican:

Vatican excommunicated Duvalier,
and with eyes, cold, unblinking, he expelled
clergy, replaced priests with priests Macoute,
evicted Jesuits... purged. Not whirlwinds

whirlwind,

    as Duvalier purged people and land, was

        reelected, unopposed—another

            six-year term, and neither invaders

nor Macoutes could cause them to curse You.

1964: U.S. President said, "This government looks forward to close cooperation and solidarity with the Government of Haiti."

Even this did not cause them to curse You.
No, not invaders, or shaking whirlwinds,
but living carnival, in festival arts
they found tom-toms, joy, radiance of sun.
Even more funds, millions, to Duvalier,
Haiti, Duvalier: minimal foreign
influence, and Haitians eclipsed, cut-off,

> ... *carried off before*
> *their time,*
> *their very foundation flowing away*
> *like a river. (22: 16)*

Not this:
1964: Duvalier: "I have a holy mission to fulfill, a mission which will be fulfilled entirely."
Nor this:
1963-68: Disasters, natural—
Hurricane Flora; Cleo, and Inez:
Duvalier called periods of national
mourning. Devastating floods—mourning
homeless—hundreds of thousands now homeless,
coffee, cattle wiped out; national
crisis, as international community gave relief,
as Duvalier declared periods
of national mourning. Their only escape—
exile, secret flight, open boat.

Not even these brought brazen blasphemy,
and curse, though none dared curse Duvalier's face:
1970: exodus—Haitian
engineers, judges, doctors, teachers,
and nurses fled to New York, Bahamas,
Burundi, Congo,
Dahomey, Guinea,
Togo, Rwanda—engineers, judges—
all unshaken, living, working
anywhere, everywhere
    but Haiti.

Duvalier's shattering, weakened frame:
1971: Dizziness, headaches, weak legs,
white-hair, unable to speak without
a slur, Duvalier proclaimed,

"That a Duvalier may one day succeed
a Duvalier   should alarm no one."
Duvalier regime survived fourteen years,
rapid insurrections   invasions   coups.

And should He stretch out His hand and touch all,
all it once had—hedged in on every side—
shall a land not curse its day of birth?
One verdant green island, once His hallowed
spot, and still, no place earthly so fruitful.

IV.
1979-82: BOAT PEOPLE FLED.
> *My harp... tuned for a dirge,*
> *my flute to the voice of those who weep.* (30: 30)

BOAT PEOPLE FLED HAITIAN CRISIS;
BOAT PEOPLE, PORT, NO PORT AWAITS.

> *My blackened skin peels off,*
> *and my body is scorched by the heat.* (30: 31)

IN WOODEN BOATS, LIPS PARCHED,
BELLIES EMPTY: **90** BOAT PEOPLE—
76 MEN, **11** WOMEN,
3 CHILDREN STRANDED, RETURNED
TO PORT-AU-PRINCE; **407** IN **60**-FOOT
WOODEN BOAT INTERCEPTED A MILE OFF
KEY BISCAYNE; COAST GUARD INTERCEPTS FREIGHTER;
200 HAITIAN IMMIGRANTS JUMP
OVERBOARD AS FREIGHTER RUNS ASHORE;
BOAT CAPSIZED, **6** HAITIANS DROWN;

> *Evil has come though I expected*
> *good;*
> *I looked for light but here came*
> *darkness...* (30: 26)

A FLOOD OF REFUGEES: **250** IN SEVERAL SMALL BOATS,
125 TRANSFERRED TO COAST GUARD VESSELS
ON AND ON; LAW HUNTED THEM, THREATENED—ANY
HAITIANS TRYING TO ESCAPE TURMOIL, VIOLENCE,
"would be turned back," said U.S. President,
said Security Council.

Not desolate hills, where mountain trees wept,
could make them fall on the ground and curse You.

PLOTS, REVOLUTIONS, OCCUPATION, INDEPENDENCE...

"The rich of my country, a tiny percentage of our
population,

sit at a vast table covered in white damask and
    overflowing with good food...
To whom the pastor gives his generous bowl of rice or
    beans,
there are a hundred thousand more..."

> *Did not he who made me in the*
> *womb make them?* (31: 15)

Tugged (as they were) by
living rendered unpredictable,
unknowable, mysterious,

through fiction, fantasy, reportage, still
their dream could not, would not surrender
to hunger, convention, blind gesture,
would not surrender even one swaying
story of life beyond plots, revolutions,
shattering sights. No, their blameless poor

began conjuring tales to be alive
with life beyond the power of the world,
alive, to be with the power which frees.

1971-90: Jean-Claude Duvalier   Leslie Manigat
    Namphy   Prosper Avril
Pascale-Trouillot... plots, revolutions, plots...

V.

Not even dreams decayed in the desert
    of hearts, dreams
which were no more than wind whistling
    through leaves; leaves... beans, coffee, leaves,
lifted and gone;

1800's planter: "The security
of the whites demands that we keep Negroes
in profound ignorance."

The Spanish, the French, colonizers—
St. Domingue—rich in sugar, cocoa, coffee,
cotton, indigo—made planters "rich
as a Creole," so the French liked to say.
The Spanish,

> *swept utterly away...*

and the French,
> *Where*
> *is he? (20: 6-7)*

Not robbers, murderers, whirlwinds that turned
land to ruin, gave personal desires
full rein, erred grievously, not even
those who had striven to improve
its condition, while their motive was their
own gain, caused the blameless to curse You.
But oh, moving forms of dust wondered,
can evanescence of being stand more,
for who can stand in the Presence of God?

VI.

Aristide promised Democracy, Aristide, who
swore no false dealings, swore the course was
not embarked on deceit, swore we could end
the trials, blood, and suffering soil of multitudes.

1988: Aristide, radio broadcast:
> "Alone we are weak.
> Together we are strong.
> Together, we are the flood..."

No, not arguments, speeches, sermons, hymns
    or deity upheld in disaster's
face, not accuser, or adversary,
    not devout or prosperous, long tested
by calamity, not the ritual
    uncleanness, or sinless perfection, not
even these agents caused numberless poor to curse,
    curse one who stood in the Presence of God.

VII.

1990: Priest, Aristide President elect. 1990: Aristide ousted by army; 40,000 boat people set sail. UN embargo Haiti: harms farmers, poor, farmers, poor—
                      touches them,
                      their toil, their soil.
"I have seen them..."
Farmers face risk, cannot sell harvest,
unable to buy food, oils, meat, beans...
from need, they bleed, plead
to a priest and leader—Aristide, his
words, wisdom, touched their black soil and toil:

> "I live in Haiti. Haiti is the parish of the poor. In Haiti, it is not enough to heal wounds, for every day another wound opens up. It is not enough to give the poor food one day, to buy them antibiotics one day, to teach them to read a few sentences or to write a few words including their name. Hypocrisy. The next day they will be starving again, feverish again, and they will never be able to buy the books that hold the words that might deliver them. Beans

and rice are hypocrisy when the pastor gives them only to a chosen few among his flock, and thousands and thousands of others starve. Oh yes, perhaps that will put the pastor's mind at rest. Hypocrisy. Because for every T. Claude, T. Bob or T. Marie to whom the pastor gives his generous bowl of rice or beans, there are a hundred thousand more T. Claudes, Bobs, and Maries, sitting on boney haunches in the dust, chewing on the pit of mango, finishing their meal for the day. I have seen them, I have seen the children the good pastor never feeds.

The rich of my country, a tiny percentage of our population, sit at a vast table covered in white damask and overflowing with good food, while the rest of my countrymen and countrywomen are crowded under the table, hunched over in the dirt and starving... a violent situation and one day the people under that table will rise up in righteousness, and... knock the table of privilege over, and take what we have all been working for all of these years in the parishes of the poor..."

1994: U.S. SENT TROOPS, 20,000 TROOPS, DEPOSED MILITARY, AND LEADER ARISTIDE RETURNED. Rousing welcome—people hail him, "Pere, Priest, Aristide," for this one said: "I have seen them, I have seen the children the good pastor never feeds."

VIII.
1492—Columbus landed at Mole St. Nicolas.
1508—Spain: sent slaves, the first African slaves to New World.
1665—Ogeron established settlement in Port-de-Paix
1679—Padrejean led first slave insurrection against French
1697—Spain conceded, yielded Western St. Domingue claim to the French—
sugarcane, indigo,
tobacco, cocoa,
cotton...

1685: Code Noir, Haiti; regulated color, legalized slavery:

Slaves may marry with master's consent.

Slaves cannot have sex with Europeans.

Slaves cannot carry weapons.

Slaves cannot hold meetings.

Slaves cannot testify against masters.

Slaves cannot leave plantations.

"The security
of the whites demands that we keep Negroes
in profound ignorance."

Slaves cannot receive education.

In St. Domingue everything takes on an air of opulence that dazzles Europeans. The throng of slaves who await the orders and even the lifted

*finger of a lone individual, confers grandeur
on him who commands them. To have four
times as many servants as one needs marks
the grandiloquence of a wealthy man... Since
the supreme happiness for a European is to be
waited on, he even rents slaves.*
    1700's, Moreau de Saint-Mery

IX.
Not Middle Passage, Hayti, St. Domingue
not invaders, arguments, or speeches,
not Macoutes, whirlwinds, or sermons caused curse,

curses from Haiti—its whole record of life—
from Africa to the West: black—mulatto,
French—Creole, Catholic—Voodoo...
plantation—subsistence farming.

"The rich of my country... sit at a vast table..."

X.
January 1, 1804: "Haiti, Independence,"
    Dessalines declared.
Dreams, dreams of democracy
from the cradle upwards.

March 1, 2004: Aristide Flies Into Exile. Declared
    Aristide: "I was forced to resign
        in a coup d' état. I was
        kidnapped at gunpoint."

Like a night vision, Aristide, target
of taunts, flown, driven away into night
the night like a dream—secret, his flight.

Washington declared:

"Absolutely absurd.

He knows what happened. He made
the right decision. Maybe he's having
second thoughts."

Reports: ARISTIDE FLIES INTO EXILE,

PROTESTORS MARCH AGAINST ARISTIDE
ARISTIDE FAILS TO DELIVER REFORMS
ARISTIDE ZERO CREDIBILITY, CAUSE OF BLOODY REVOLT.

Contradictory reports.

A report, name, vague name: J.B. Like Job,
suffering righteous, tradition of suffering;
remnant of people in captivity:

Taino Indians, African slaves.

Africa: Angola, Congo, Dahomey,
Guinea, Senegal, Sudan, all brought to
"Hayti," greatest colony of France once;

ten million slaves—ten million
brought to the New World,
and
    I alone escaped to tell the tale (1: 15)

Land of the Mountains—refuge,
refugees scattered as chaff, sails, winds, winds
   from homeland; taken; led away;

tell the tale of affliction, not cause
cause of life's unraveling, sifting of
Providence and a war with heaven, grief,
loss—tempestuous reply. But if I knew,

if cause I knew,
it's gone now, sacrificed all on an altar,
wind, excesses, reduced to silence.

XI.
Man learns his lesson on a bed of pain…

Take care not to turn to mischief;
for that is why you are tried by
affliction. (36: 21)

Affliction— colonialism
         — dictatorship
         — inherited despotism
         — failing democracy
         — military rule
sorrow upon sorrow, and arrows
of trial…

By divining to know what made them so blue,
the orphans and victims now many, not few,
    have known affliction, flood of afflictions:
Affliction of knife, sword, gun, bomb—
their clouds have grown thick, and their nights are
    long,
weeping silence, impenetrable fears,
    for Insistent Self neither sees nor hears
the outcast, widow, aged or child
in lands grown fertile, now untended—grown wild.

Stripped like a vine, shattered and broken
by wounds as wide as oceans, pour out
your heart, oh Jewel of the Caribbean,
pour out tears till they become stars, splendor
and light:
    Oh nations and people,
from afflicted hearts,
lamentation and anguish.
Oh Giver,
to multitudes,
    multitudes
of dismay and distrust,
agony, wreckage, and still
they call, Oh Open of Hand,
    they call, Oh Blessed Protector
Oh Loving Kind Helper,
O Bountiful Radiance
    of Shining Dominion

save us.

Crepusculo

Whether it was Antietam or Sharpsburg,
we drove by stalks silent as headstones and

acres of green. Our first trip South, and I
wanted to see battles only heard of.

"This ain't nothin' but corn," you said as a
crowd listened to our guide, a boy maybe

sixteen or so, who meant to make July heat
bearable; his voice speaking faster, till all was

lost in tide of words that you say, "Jus' means
a lot of people died right about harvest time."

At Bloody Lane we could see how all
of it happened when tall stalks buried

voices behind rows, rows and rows of green,
and all I saw was your mother's kitchen

where she spends days canning, saying,
"These jars come in handy if war happens.

I'll never forget the Depression." Jars—
yellow, red, green, in neat tidy rows, rows

like cornfields ready for harvest. Her voice,
"Remember this, remember that"— taught you

how to live off berries for weeks. While in
this soil, I see nothing of the old black

who looked like your mama or mine hollerin'
out a back door: "They tol' us that lan' would

be ours, and they lied. They tol' us we have
rights and schools for the child'en, an' they lied;

an' maybe we ain't nev'r gon' be free cause
free ain't no place in partic'lar—jus' a

way to be." When I consider how their
light was spent, after that trip, I never

told you that if nuclear war happened
I just could not imagine, imagine

anything but stillness and suffering,
the groaning as smoke cleared, and we were not

dead, just wounded amid rows, rows of corn
ready for harvest. When I consider

how each light is spent: Chavez says he
will never give up *his* Presidency
in Venezuela: (like Aristide did)

> Josephina crouched inside a dirt doorway, back
> to wall, afraid to lift her head where shots bring
> screams to silence. When they found her, all she
> could say was the voices in the street sounded
> like a tree fullofbirdsatreefullofbirdsatreefull

Toes and knees pressed against cool dark earth as
she thinks already in the street outside our house
is the ghost of a dead policeman. She wonders if
he is really dead or just pretending since his gun
is still warm and the smooth dark club ready to
drum heads that break like melons, or bodies that
look like mattresses her mother made from stray
piles of clothing.

And your mother shelves jars while something of
life, death, remains elusive. And how far

this cornfield seemed from us weeks later, when
we came to a green field, no marble

or monument to those who'd been a world
of tears. Again, I thought of the cornfield—

stalks bent by wind became men, reeds blowing
in winds, and then, rows of bodies reaped, stacked

one upon another till the crooked
rails of Bloody Lane became bin walls, but

no sign from age-old blacks warning, "Be
faithful, be watchful Jacob, for the word

can come and give no understandin', the
crooked word is killin'; be careful," they

whispered again and again. When I see
how their lives were spent, full night and sunrise

kneading life into another consistency,
perhaps here was the wisdom of Jonah

in the belly of a whale, Daniel in
a pit, or Harriet Tubman running

in darkness with those who could feed only
upon night become more real, more real than

the ocean's strength, lion's jaw, or a path
marked by danger, peril, hidden hazards:

> Seething, shattering blasts in Baghdad and
> numerous bodies and body parts,
>
> multiple explosions in Karbala,
> call for blood, mosques calling people, call
>
> for blood transfusions, call for blood—
> problem, a problem in metaphysics.

Yes, when I consider how our light is
spent, twilight is the wisdom of each who

has learned to look upon darkness and know
one more story within story until

telling is a bible of sorts and all
griots—Cassandra. Crepusculo and

life enmeshed like lovers. And of that Lane,
those fields, you're right, *This ain't nothin' but corn.*

Job's Wife Speaks

If He would slay me, I should not hesitate;
I should still argue my cause to His Face. JOB, 13: 15

And do you suppose *our* house is tended
well, while others look on in relief, like
sparrows or birds of pity, like they
have to make a go of it. Neighbors,
now say, "Nahrela, why don't you throw—

throw a little get together to cheer
him, get his mind off these troubles?" but
they're thinking, "Nahrela, why don't you pray
he'll leave it all to you so you can start
again?" Of course, I am overlooked, *your*

wife, who gave you ten children before all
these disasters, your wife who's lost faith in God
from Job's itching, worms, running sores, fevers,
his blackened skin—and his face, shining face—
no longer the man, man from Uz— man I

married, and you now wishing you'd
never been born! And our servants running
away, cursing. Our own sons, and the graceless
sons of those you've counseled once, saying
to all—me: "he's sinned—dead—he's turned away.
He's God's forgotten, God's forsaken letter."

Then last night, you asked bitter darkness, "Why,"
and I say, *"Aye,"* but to me, *me*—your wife,
you say, "Nahrela, He's our God. Even
if He slay me, I should not hesitate;
I should defend my cause to His Face." And

storming in anger, I say, *"Go ahead,
curse God and die!"* I mean, that's what you want,
and my prayer is not a wall or fence, protecting
our house from limitless grief. Even
this brought no change in you. Tearful I asked,

And what am I to say to our daughters,
tell them that love has no eyes, no pain,
current or tide? Or say, Pay no mind to things
under this mourning river: husband, land,
your family, servants, and friends who've

come to see night fallen, a fallen star?
This is tedious talk, but don't get me wrong,
I am not sour or bitter from the
way I am muted, simply called your wife;
I suppose it's an oversight to all

the confusion plaguing us. But I am
perplexed, puzzled by us and our issue.
I mean, do you suppose we can talk of sweet
things in a house grown quiet when night falls,
and you, lying speechless as a newborn

babe with nothing on your tongue but tears?
And your mother, her crying, calling me
to *do something,* anything to comfort
you in your losses, your losses? as though I
was a well full of water—or mine of jewels.

And when those three came and stayed,
for seven days sat silent vigil,
looking, praying for you every night and
every sunrise, "Your houses," they said, "must
be offered up, sons and all, as reasons,"

not comforting; never wise words from them.
So it's true; I have no hope, but I will defend
my ways, and consider what to say now,
here in this empty, joyless house: I know
unearthly scenes may pass with time or death,

but the life you choose, like one chosen for
you shall be, without question or remorse,
endured. Hope for end, end to it all when
tears fly to exile, and we can live our
last days in peace, flourishing.

Mengele

Dear Halvah Leah,

With such news, you will feed this city.
Each night I see them in the stars; from every
nation, city and district, a sea of faces.
And I know God's greatness is giving
the impossible to the most unlikely.

Since you wrote last, I have been to the beach
every day: yesterday was a moon-tide,
waters rose, I tell you, higher than the tide
of first love. I watched seaweed dropped
like bad memory at shore's edge.

I thought of your news: on February
5th, he took a bus to Bertioga;
on February 7th, he went to the sea.
The beach seemed so peaceful till then.
You say he was not washed ashore but

lifted, pushed by two hands trying to save
him from a pointless bus ride? In seaweed
I see two hands holding him above crests
meant to cool his body frying in heat
of a sweltering Brazilian summer.

So. Even here on this beach, far
from ovens of flesh, hair, far from gas
on the left, living on the right, his family
joy-rides and friends of the society,
I see him. You know, I have never learned

to swim. To let my body float, float
in anything on earth that does not anchor
is too much: so much life taken, from us,
taken from us. But then, there is some comfort
in knowing that two hours from bungalow

5555 Alvenenga Road and twenty-five
miles south of Sao Paulo, he rode
the water's edge, till six million hands,
till seaweed pulled him back from another
shore of escape, and two hands could not save

him from those sent by the Angel of Death
to yet another Maker! Still, you do
not change, and our speech brings me back
where we meet face to face, and speak
syllable for syllable—unions

that bear no exchange like foreign coins:
something higher for something lower.
No, Leah, even now as we breathe
all is open. Open, write soon,

Miriam

Seedling Remembrance

In the seed a universe is with us,
whole, where watchers
      find the tree, blossom or leaf,
the potential, potency
      of seed—sun, soil, dew—
divinity of hyacinth or rose,
      remembrance complete.

And we shall be as leaves upon the tree
whose roots are to earth deeply married, whose
      branches, in all kinds of weather,
free-reach toward sky,

and when the falling time comes,
we shall not weep for things unbound;
      winds more tender
than breezes of love's boasting

have freed us. Mastered by love, we
become another season's flaming color,
      move-on toward long-lasting fields
covered in myrtle and favored by the gods.

Pangaea

I.
Plates moving—dive, shift at mid-ocean ridge,
opening rifts; earth's mantle welling up
    new stuff, seething, splitting, nature's boundary,
volcanic—quakes, nature's lines—
    while plate slides past plate, shearing,
    spewing
splitting into island and drift. Moving
    plates—embedded continents—land awakens.

II.
Call it a death ring, say, God passes by
shrouded in cries of a people who flee,
a people adrift when skies open wide
as rivers, so full they wash all into
hurricane's eye, hidden crusts, ruptures,
turning-under.

What of this worldly dream all dream, or us?
No silken tent for refugees spread, so
the letter goes on this ruinous soil...
Bosnia, Somalia, Israel, Sumatra,
tsunami—Indian Ocean shores,
hundreds of thousands dead, missing,
America shaken, shaken like leaves—
North, East, South, West.

III.
Earth, air, sky, waves kill, hoe unseen,
as fires fume, sizzle, smoking peaks—beauty,
    annihilation.

IV.
Nothing but harrowing accounts, exiles
strange as Pharaoh's, a harvest of sorrow,
and canticles of grief for all dark skies
of locusts and flies, billowing as sheets
in wind—like sheets on a mother's clothesline.

Noonsigns

Setting: a rural, Southern town; a young man approaches an old woman, Sarah, seated on her porch; he notices a town celebration and asks Sarah: "What's the celebration about?" She responds, "Schoolteacher died." He asks, "Then why are they celebrating?" And Sarah said—

I.
She had always said, "Sarah, it's a delicate
thing, students passing through hands."
And she called us by name when she had something
for us to think about. The first day, she had candles.
She brought one for everyone in that class;
she made us take one and hold it in front
like we were praying. When it was quiet, she
lit her candle, and started talking. She said
that each one of us—our minds—were candles
waiting to be lit, but we wouldn't get lit, unless
we brought our candles to hers, since we were
students with no matches on hand. And she said
it was a give and a take, a humbling in giving,
and a humbling in taking, but once lit,
we'd burn on our own. And she loved colors.
You could say that's how she saw each student.
They were precious. Oh, not because she
got to know their business or their private
ways—but special because, if she'd been an
artist, a painter, they'd have been her paints—
each one a different color, and she
was just the brush.
(laugh)

When mine were in school, they said
it was enough to know: 1+1 was 2.
Learning was basic reasoning and facts,
facts... Facts. Said it was *enough?!?*
But you and I know: this life, it's not
reasonable and that's not enough...
not enough at all!

So in teaching facts, she *meant* to make
you *wonder!* Wonder about the wilderness
between failure and hope. Spaces!
She taught you how to fill in the spaces.
Oh, she could give plenty of facts, but
she'd say, "They're slippery things, Sarah—
Too many, and the mind dries up like unused
paints... a world with no texture. Too little
fact, and we are diluted and deluded,
and it's sad to see minds without a purpose—
as if it isn't clear already that the mind
was meant to expand! We'd be strange
boxes otherwise, huh Sarah?" And I'd just nod
feeling she knew because she'd been wondering
longer.

II.

The day was hot and dry. It was noon.
That sun was bright orange against cloudless
blue. The night before, it rained hard, and the
passing came late. Still, the service was attended
by most of the community. And it
was a day for children: they came dressed in
different colored dresses and suits. A life
come and gone. And a candle was lit and
passed around for each one to light his own.

And remembering the kind of life she
had lived, some folks, feeling it was a sign
opened their Bibles to pray. Well Mister,

I've been here 43 years. Belle worked like
a Master: "Sarah?" She'd say, "it's enough
to make you wonder, students passing through
hands, delicate hands; it's such a slippery
slippery thing."

Song

Lovers speak in measured words that do not
    batter and clang upon the ears like bad
horns, but words that are a clarion call,
    mighty commanders, longing to conquer
the lying world with the fiery heart
    and charming applause, a charming
that frees all delicate maidens' second
    thoughts about love and men's tempting glances.
Lunatic, they run through valleys, groves
    dark forests, love blind with love that can't keep
a secret, to sing these bright gifts of Jove: feasts
    brimming with gleaming cups, ointments, sweets,
garlands, meats—*Go slow!* Love shines like the moon,
    a bright constellation for voyagers,
so who should come first in its song? You, like
    a clear-voiced flute, over and over.

To the Aquarium, Brighton Beach

The day we went to the aquarium
we rode the train with an English woman
whose hands moved like one knitting—no needles,
no yarn, or like birds, wings pressing air,
and I asked myself, did she find what she went to see?

She was swimming in joy like the dolphins
as she shared the tale of her day, and I
kept wondering, did she find what she went
to see, she whose bags were filled with remnants,
and whose hands moved with the grace of dancers?

Primer

In memory of Dr. Doris Ray Adler

Hands. eyes. mouth. nose. teeth,
smile. Knees, ankles, feet,
walked. At two, I learned
my alphabet. My
hands. My feet. My face.
My teeth, nose, eyes, on
and on. I recited words
out loud then found the shape—
matching like socks. Each
sound, a mirror,
like pant legs, always two:
two eyes, two hands, two lips—one mouth
speaks and learns, learns things are
as they exist. And my compact
vocabulary builds dictionaries I must
abandon, forget in another season,
when births of spirit teach the body
that things are not only as they exist:
   Simile, symbol, metaphor, irony.
I know now that I am born
to lose my body—only, not memories shared
with you, dearest comrade—
smiles, evoked from heart's hidden stirrings
   move like leaves in wind—and if lucky,
I learn we are born, contingent, born to a new
Alphabet of knowing, ancient and sacred,
   learn gardens, whose blossoms
are not here only, but blooming
invocations to Invisible Becoming,

Unknowable Being. And so this
is all I am now, friend: poetry, spirit,
      and prayer: My eyes, my hands,
mouth...
      Clothed by your love,
I walk back into Eden, unafraid.

Luna

On nights like this, some conjure images:
pale horse, pale rider. On such nights as these,

sweet Juliet apprises Romeo,
"Swear not by the moon," and Kate complies

to Petruchio, "it is the sun, it is
the blessed moon." Luna—mantle of rock,

denser than crust thirty-seven miles in
thickness; one small, iron core surrounded

by molten zone; surface densely cratered,
mountainous highlands, and large circular

smooth-floored plains called *maria*. But before
men in metal helmets planted flags, or spoke

timeworn syllables: "One small step for Man,"
we were much closer to lunar music.

Since then, few notice the milky softness
of moon; even lovers look to other signs

for the blush of love, ever palpable
now, altered by peering. But in Haiti,

hearts touch moon, light bends, broken and broken
again on the sea, nights open in the

peeling of mangoes. And moon reigns wherever
magical touch remains, while astonished

eyes wonder—mystery: that so little
should have taken us to the moon back then.

Gathering

      Years of gathering,
gathering years and books of religion,
philosophy, history, tales of faith,
gender, race, myths, and flights of grace
until the shelves, the shelves are full.

And soon these too recede, and only one
line will be left to memory, being,
only one line engraved upon heart like
chrysolite—luminous letters—poetry,
felt only in gathering, for that is all

all there is when years have fallen away:
childhood, maturity and old age, like
another page turned in love's windblown book,
as all autumn turnings fall away: tears,
exaltation. All! Surely we're letters

in the book each heart is writing, reading,
and then discarding to forgetfulness
or time, or to those who live after fire
and gold, who light love's tablets in a night
of veils to dream and wake, waking

to evanescence of being, souls, souls
eternally freed from gravity and bone.

Climbing

In magic of stars, arch of sky
I climb this wind-weathered stone, travel
where silence is edge beneath rock's roundness—
and footholds, handholds carefully placed,
I stop where all hangs above land bound
things to gaze once more at place where we live—
where outbreaks occur, picking up pieces,
picking up pieces where sirens live and
crushing devastation, cause of our woes.
Eyes rise to surmount the unmapped country
of gusts and storms to look for a clean line
in rock, this stone that bears my weight.

Birth

And so you begin, you begin your flow.
And may it be full of wonder, joy in flow

of breathing, seeing, and touching,
knowing what it is to be alive, what

it is to live upon this land, dreaming
of stars and mountains, rivers and oceans,

rain forests, woods, as glorious waters
open and fall to spirit moving

in you, clear spirit, and love's ocean brought
forth—heart, where hidden birds in full trees

forever sing mystic dreams, flow,
and sacred river, flow of all rivers

which have come before.

Seed the Unbroken Land

Soul, the unbroken land,
ever in need,
turning, digging
to bear a seed,
hoe, shovel, fork, rake—
some turn soil, some take root
hope heart will bear
seed's sweetest fruit.

The Man From Virginia

And for the season, it was winter...Besides, what could they see but a hideous and desolate wilderness, full of wild beasts and wild men.. and the whole country, full of woods and thickets... a wild and savage hue.
       William Bradford, OF PLIMOUTH PLANTATION, 1620

I.
An intense People of the Book, Pilgrims
named others strangers, sailed to strange land,
called themselves saints, pursued a dream
eyes full—passion, water, water had been
enough after three months—and they longed
for land where they could take hold and root,
root on stone, and feared woods—its dangerous silence.

1996, Upstate, New York
One night we were sitting in the house, my wife and
me; we were in the living room, kids asleep and bang,
it come right through the window and landed in the
wall. Right from the wooded Oak and Pine, bang!
We replaced eight windows this year; we'll replace
a lot more. It's scary; it's a game to those kids, an
addiction—if you get a gun, shoot it or it's no fun.

II.
1998, Americana

Today, you cannot stop by woods, even
on snowy evenings, and those who live there
think it queer to find a place where one can
hear the lovely, silent wood. On
the broken tree line broken by shots, a
neighbor cries, **I'm tired of hearing guns;**
I'm tired of hearing gun practice; I'm

tired of hearing of neighbors' kids dying.
I wouldn't walk in the woods for anything;
there's always somebody with a gun or
kids shootin' animals: squirrels, birds,
cats, target practice; we've lost four cats and
my friend down the road just lost his dog! Just
kids wanting to kill something... if you shoot
targets... no challenge, no power; for them,
it's a shootin' passion.

III.
Glimmer—a flash recalls our darkest nights: **December 1st, 1997, Paduchah, Kentucky: Boy wearing a gun, concealed. Three girls shot and killed at school.**

IV.
The son recalls,

> "He laid down the law, my father. He was
> one of the great men; where are the great ones
> now? OK sure, we were poor, but I niver
> felt it then. On the porch, my daddy, 'fore
> he'd go hunting, he'd take a few steps, then
> he stop, look into them woods, spit and
> clap his hands, 'That's good,' he say, 'the hunt, the
> beauty of it, emotion... it's there, hangs,
> even in mist.' Yes sir, my daddy, he laid
> down the law, and I tell you his calling
> had a law an' order of its own."

V.
1990, Princeton, New Jersey

A bus stop. Five laughing black boys full of
themselves, young teens, moved with ease to back

of bus, taking up an entire seat.
For now, they forget girls. 1963, too young
to march, four young girls in a Birmingham
church died singing God's praises, girls, singing
for the right to sit anywhere on the bus.
Among complacent whites, the boys took
no notice, did not notice they were five
of only six blacks riding. Boys, youths, who
took no one into account—just silence.

Robert, oldest, biggest, was first to speak
the word's unsheathed weapon, "Maan, I sure
do hate me some god damn white people; the mother
fuckers stink!" From the back seat, like a wave
rushing from shore to shore, boys' laughter filled
the bus; boys pleased with cool cockiness.
Jarryd was next, "And they're uuugly too."
Laughter. Keith joined the choir, "I'd like
to kill 'em all, but it'd be a waste
of good bullets." Uproarious laughter.
Maurice—quiet one, made bold by silence
of intended targets, added his piece, "They
make me want to puke." Inspired words—
their power, magic—never miss the mark.

1963, four young girls, a Birmingham church,
died singing God's praises, singing for the
right to sit anywhere on the bus.

At first, no one saw the old man shuffling
to the back, shopping bag in hand, movement
as deliberate as it was steady, slow.
Facing the boys, he reached into his
bag and pulled out the gun, shining metal,
its silence was enough; pointedly he aimed

the barrel toward each boy, and calmly spoke,
"I want all you niggers back here to shut
up. Understand? I want all you niggers,"
gun pointed, word for word, at them—
"to shut up!"

Cocky ones cock the guns, cockatoo
cockatoo. Click, cock, click cock; life measured
not in coffee spoons, but clicks and cock.

**March, 1998, fire alarm pulled. From a wooded
area, two boys, 11 and 13, shots like firecrackers:
Jonesboro, Arkansas: "This is rural Arkansas, guns
are part of the family norm. We've never had a
problem before." Dead, four girls, one teacher. A
local minister weeps, recalls how he held the dying
girl's hand.**

Darkness drops, **1999: Columbine.**

VI.
"I'm OK. I'm solo in charge. Ok-k-k-la
Ok-lahoma, men ignite this bomb, know—
be innocent flower and serpent under it."

VII.
Memory, flash,

his daddy's words "Out here, we're not dying,
we put life into dying... There will be
time, Yes sir boy, time for you, time for me."
Son's memory—failings, solitary successes,
the healing gun—and Daddy's words.

Now he walked silently, missing effect,

but never its mark: recalling action,
a man concealing his gun, always
on his body the gun, his communion
became union with living and dead:

"Go git that gun boy, and be quick!"
When his father spoke, the boy knew
to move, move like he was on fire.

VIII.

An old hunting dog at rest in the corner,
knows the sound of gun-getting, and soon

he's up, muscles taut, ready to hunt woods,
familiar scents; his keen eyes no longer

match aging body, but he could
bark bark bark like a son-of-a-gun;

nothing escapes his gaze or nose
for fearful, haunted prey.

And a boy was honored; his father
had never before trusted his

son's young fingers with this prized
possession, whose power remained

concealed, most of the time, like the gun
in a pine box, or poised on a rack.

Always loaded, the gun sat waiting
like a lover to be held and drawn

close in hands who knew its secrets, power.
Something was shared between gun and

father who carried it, slung over his
shoulder, like a backpack full of books.

And the boy moved—as instinctively
as dog—toward the case, opened it

and pulled *Baby* out of its cradle;
then he moved toward his father,

clippety clop clickety clop, and boy
didn't even remember his feet

touching the floor; he was watching
his father's face, expressionless,

but the body sure in movement. Soon,
they were out the door, and dusk held them,

held them—father, boy and dog—
bodies sealed shut as envelopes,

and movement—wooden, unbothered
by people. Boy was seven and

that's all he, a man himself now,
could recall of the father, the hunt.

He was boy safe from woods' hidden
danger, and on that day, when his father

took him hunting for the first time,
boy held *Baby's* magic and mystery,

the fog and mist in evening approach.
"Git the dog off the leash," said his father,

man of few words, and dog—barking
already. Boy, fearful of missing

meaning concealed, urgent command,
moved fingers quickly; boy wanted

father to see reflex release chain,
wanted father to see him as reflex,

unconscious thought, *see* boy made real
in rhythm of dog, of father—(clippity clop).

A father's features, now a son's whole soul.
It would be a great hunt through mist.

Boy, reactions automatic as gun,
and loaded with feeling. Deeply moved,

the boy spoke, "We gonna get
rabbit or deer today?" Slow to

respond, the father focused, was transformed
by mist, became son's teacher-poet, saying,

IX.
"Today you become a man.   We're not hunting
for anything.   Today you're gonna learn to shoot
Baby
          an' then   when you're ready   we'll hunt.
There's a lot a boy's gotta learn   first.
You an' *Baby* got to git aquainted   smell her   feel
her   every gun's
          got a way
an' you got to make it work   *your way*.   Stuff you
gotta know first.   Like how to get a target in your
sights, how to aim *Baby*   an' when you pull the
          goddamn trigger
how to man the kick   *Baby's* got a kick, you know,
she ain't like a woman   givin' up something for

nothin'   that's somethin' you gotta know
if you want *Baby* to work for you   an' stay in charge.

That's what I'm teaching you, boy   how to stay in
charge   Man's gotta stay in charge in this world
or it all goes to shit, right to hell
          white man's got more to lose these days
an' don't you forget I told you that   this baby is your
protection   your right   to bear   arms
an' protect what's yours.

We done lost   more than I care to think about   but
now   I'm teaching you what   those first sons-of-bitches
knew who came to this country
Claim it, an' protect it with your life   God's country?
Shaaah   by God we took it an'   *ain't* gonna give it
back   without *somebody* paying an ass whippin'
an' that's that.

          You hear me boy?   Where ever you go in life,
you remember what I told you
an' if someone gits smart   or tries to take your natural
man's rights,   you
may die in the fight,   but make sure they know who
           you were,   hear me?
You're the man from Virginia, one of the few states
where a white man still has claiming rights.
You're *the man*
                    from Virginia!"

Odysseus in the Underworld

Shade, faithful to light and memory's crystal
draught, shade—a spirit speaking a wine
of utterance for kindred, hidden secrets.

Her shadowy fingers pointed towards
you, fingers longing one peerless embrace.
And Odysseus, three times, three times

your mother and you rush to embrace
—each desperate to hold the other—

and each time, her shadowy spirit sifts—
a dream or branch with falling leaves. She,

rib less, amidst rustling shades' darksome night,
knows sinews no longer bind. In sorrow,

all your mother could say was "You must long
for the daylight. Go quickly." Torn away,

how you longed to touch her, touch
your own fleeting darkness, as

she offered love's only words, "My shining
Odysseus." So in this—underworld—you

learn why localized within scaffold
and center of frame, of bone, is eye,

ear, nose, tongue; you learn to bind this world—
home, and above—discover, discern,

forbear and incline, pour out and bear
what surrounds you in stillness or sound. From

touch, everywhere spread over your skin, you
learn to praise, proclaim creation's secret

offering: to feel, embracing all your loves,
their unceasing call to gathering seas, where all

all is not shell.

Toward the Silence

> For Robert Hayden

For poets, words grow in darkness toward the silence
 of light.
A door opens telling them, more than one way, more
 than one room.
Your composure, filled with the knowledge of
 entrances,
ever-mindful of a singular exit. Poet, a man near blind,
clasping metaphors that give sight, vision. When we
 first

met you, it was winter. You seemed to hate snow that
 made
things one color, texture, one bitter cold feeling. You
spoke of the whiteness that had caused a taxi to lose
its way in city sea, and this day, you were late to class.
Still we waited, waited to learn. And in February, with
 spring

approaching, you left us—not winter, not fall, not
 summer—
spring. A new world emerges when death becomes the
 call,
forging order, order that is mine. And that first winter,
I watched you place hands in Hayden pockets to keep
 warm,
and you gave a prophecy:

- the reasons for poetry: life, and to hold the deaf
 till they hear the word love.

- there is no speech barrier, just a people grown hard of hearing, people with no hands, useless eyes... non-believers.

- poetry, like life, is mystery, but mystery that cannot lose all ties, all links to our being. Symbol was not enough to join winter to spring; non-believers need more...

And through the cold, confusion, we learned. Learned
that our past, hidden in numberless cries—Middle
     Passage—
was not just ours, but every beings'; that heritage was
     theirs
also, and you said, a new world order would come
     when
our death became the call forging *universal* order.

Now it is spring, and I have become a lady of the
     subway,
riding trains is not my hobby, it's my life, and the words
you left have become a ray of sun, light—keeping
winter away. And today, this lady of the subway thinks
of you, and watches broken fragments of passing life

moving toward the silence to learn that death is not
a future stop, nor like these faces, a lasting impression.
And sometimes, sometimes memory is enough.
Poet, man, teaching us to know a meaning in
worship, the word, you knew pain, silence,

and shade of beauty. You left us in spring, and
earth put on a new garment with your passing.
So we watch the memory of your being,
ever wary of a peculiar ascent—an angle of vision,
pulsating warmth. You, who came to us in winter,

and left in spring, of you,
memory is enough to bridge winter to spring.
Feeling your presence still, and yes, memory is enough.
This time, memory is enough.

Running the Big River

Put in: above a tributary from Mexico,
    above cross canyons.
Take out: where Rio Grande is called wild, scenic,
where help is several hours or days away,

and as others, to ride, realize river another way.
River moving between rocks,
    canyons, mood and power,
as last hill above floodplain fades from view,

as something breaks, as loose-drifted sand
disappears, it's just river, taking all
    past yuccas, great stalks where white flowers
    cluster,
past tree tobacco's brilliant yellow blooms,

blooms favoring hummingbirds. Mystery river,
river where eyes fail, fail to comprehend largess, and
    thought
    caught in momentary eddies, becomes silence
floating toward something like prayer or longing to see
    life

that is different: turtle, spotted frog, river dove
or beaver become blessings breaking upon heart,
    longing to know one is not alone in the Big Bend,
hoping for hidden spaces and heart, yearning

to see coyote track, javelina, mountain lion, or
the brave, who first bore this heat and fled its floods
    to praise Hooded Oriole's golden crown
and white wingbars—one splash

of color in a green floodplain. Where canyons cry out,
currents move like mighty waters, and where waters
    go slack, slack as a bow, streams run down
to thistle, bramble, dry gullies' overflow.

Wish you could close your eyes, close your eyes to see
in mid-air flight ducks and falcons floating upstream,
    more certain of direction than you or I. Close your
    eyes
and wilderness opens: cattle, carcass, flies,

flood-crests, deposits, silt—before boundaries
of private, separate lives,
    before footsteps tracing lands invisible from shore;
I wish you could close your eyes and see,

sharp bends and big grassy
vegas where all rests, then moves on
    to a good, warm spring, accessible only
where waters are medium or low.

Above the river, sandstone and limestone
weathered red; mottled rock and patches of cane
    hide the black-necked garter and rattler.
Above waters' way through, cliffs tower,

cliffs, running into Uplands, their various names,
    similar
names, confusing features, and here, even maps
    fail as living river, carved by water, gravity,
heat and cold is river living in the Big Bend.

Where the cave invites or caves call, it's
only you, it's you in a country of spirits,
      spirits whose dance done once upon towering
bluffs, made rocks slide, falls and channels, arroyos,

and warm springs rising from the bank
by a grove of cottonwood trees. So life is here,
      and so strange that miles from others,
in this river, water, to come to know

all as flow—each of us traveling 'midst hidden
      dangers,
each choosing a Rio Grande with walls
      of various names, confusing features,
where there too, a canyon rises from a riverbank,

scarred and fractured in places, rises from the bank,
from a river of weapons and Arms, where beauty or
      mystery
      disappears, and only pour-offs, rapids,
and violent eddies command our eyes.

And now, having floated the soul's rugged
lower canyon, made the entire run in canyons,
      canyons
where choice is rare, in this: one human river

crashing beneath us on rocky, stony hearts,
do we portage, make camp
      or simply go raging in flow, content
with taking out far down river in wilderness

of dangerous crossings? Or do we move
to warm springs: hearts' longing for life that's different,
     full of living and blessing, streams—souls
praying we're not alone?

And wonder this, do we see city as desert,
missing mystery or hummingbird flight?
     Out there in the Big Bend, choice is rare
and canyons say mostly *it's river flow.* In the end,

flow will decide, only flow.

Map Reading

Heraclitus thought all things went back
to the first, a man, obsessed by change, he saw
everything in a state of flux. Stoics
sought something more lasting: virtue only

good, vice only ill, and so the only
happiness—to comply with nature: line
with nature is line with reason is line
with God. And who could not yield to their line

of thought, their ways, the clear cut of reason
through obscurity, through passion, answer to
screaming surf, rising sun, myth of clouds?
The vague mythologies gone. Direction.

Maps, lots of lines—like looking at Earth
from space, was like finding place or home
or earthly direction—east, west—boundaries
imagined, boundaries made; longitude,
latitude, limits you know like sun's
rising and setting, iridescent light
setting rising illimitable light.
"Line with nature is line with reason is
line with God, this only is Good."

Maps from moon to Mars—land maps, ocean maps,
sky-maps—flight, designated direction,
and I never was good at reading them.
Destination, *Road Map to Peace*, teenage
boy, bombs strapped to body, crosses from
Palestine, borders beyond, points to map
promising seventy-two virgins, cries,
"I did not want to die, did not want to die."

The blossoming world or life you live—
a map, artifact, and problem of mirrors.
Map, it's space, eternity's glow
and woeful winds always at one's elbow.
Heaven or hell, unbearable axis
one curving space, continuum to time
where we glimpse, not love or rest, glimpse
only grief's memories. Light, where
nothing lives or lasts past flux, reflection,

entangled jungles crawling with life
and loss, where the angle or its refraction—
map made—is search for *the word* or good life
in diary, art, letter or force of
uncontrollable acts, lines of approach—
"line with nature is line with reason is
line with God, this only is Good."

In life of lines is the spirit entwined.

Worlds from Babel, Two Towers, 9/11

These fragments have I shored against my ruins...
The Peace which passeth understanding.
                                        T.S.Eliot

Knowing how one makes the acquaintance
    of those who do not figure conspicuously
in history, whose strong appeal is meeting
    them more than once, and the meeting,
largely a matter of chance. There are
    lives only parts of which remain alive, born
from obscurity of struggle worth having.
    So. We cannot draw the line, more,
something more than a number, more
    than the sum of parts—nothing
so simple as that in the end, but something
    common between them,
not a poem but a whole book to be sung
    and sung, shared till even
the planet itself is freed from killing grip,
    and born from the tragedies of ruinous worlds,
the Ideal world—takes form.

A Sacred Geometry

For Julie Badiee

...Or consider our science of numbers,
a language of proportion and form,
precise measurements of things
(celestial, terrestrial) where the Names of God,

are also exact position and variations,
and the tradition of Geometria,
each Name of God is number, sign,
perfection, whose numerical value teaches
the curve of spirit and the line of mind.

So was the universal language Pythagoras knew:
a canon of spiritual proportions,
for geomancers, an ideal ordering numerical,
geometric design in figure and line,

arithmetic and plan in Mind Divine:

Twelve labors, twelve signs, twelve disciples, tribes;
four seasons, four directions, four evangelists,
the Quadrivium; seven planets, seven ages,
seven virtues, vices, seven days and climes;

nine Hindu mandalas, nine elements,
the Greatest Buddha, Baha, and Dante too
preferred the fineness of nine. Nine circles
of hell, nine heavens of Paradise.

Five senses, five fingers, the pentagram's tale,
three days in the tomb or the belly of whale,
an affinity for Trinity—points or lines to divinity.
God geometrizes Design divine,

While passions ascending by threes, fours,
sevens, nine, twelve, while heavens'
crypt-icon shapes are numberless stars,
are numerical keys to the sacred geometry

Of all terrestrial things—
an Order begun in One,
one never-ending universe.

Florence

I.
Nothing once absorbed is wholly lost. In
lowlands, they built castles, fought mighty wars,
as youths, wrote verses to the past, and bid
a sound farewell to the old Age; they were
joy and song and beauty crowned. Now statue
eyes are dreaming, dreaming, turning moonlight
into noon, silence, and words—windlasses
casting about the calm, a fair city
where the lute was never silent—spring-tide,
summer, and the star, star of poetry
unblemished "went up, and filled the heavens
                    with light."

II.
Hidden somewhere below mountain river,
lost itself for a season underground
in unexplored ravines: carnivals and
poems, paintings, sculpture, waters' gentle
streams. The old would peel words like fruit: baskets
of them—apples, bananas, oranges—
seek life's strange blend of tenderness, regret,
seek strength, and yearning, strong-ache and beauty.
For old ones know and remember living
is nothing without the rind, or perhaps,
divine it's easier to paint like Giotto
than recall lost phrases of love.

Petrarch: Another Earthly Conflict

When the moon holds sway, and sun
sleeps in a mystical veil of a thousand

paradises, a poet knows offerings
should be made to good fires and warm

chambers. Fountains flow beyond glory, love, fortune
and a poet refines, knows beauty's song,

knows one cannot pour wine, new
and divine, into old bottles.

Boccaccio

Sketch, survey, oh he could sing them.
A disappointed monk, or Francesca's
episode; tragic love; gay, youthful men,
hero shepherds. Geomancy—designs,
designs drawn as geometrically
as a church by Brunelleschi.

Dying for Religion

From dawn of history stood the Divine
root of the soul, fruit of the vine.

Perennial Source calls forth human course—
the stars, planets—with Unknowable Force,

geometrical ornament, nothing interferes,
exalting Deity, all disappears:

each human face, or peacock's cry,
the stoic's step, love's gazing eye—

each spirit born to spirit spent
searches the half-lights where Spirit went,

its glimmer and shadow, mystery, strife,
circumstance, image—full waters of life.

In dawn of history stood the Divine
root of the soul, fruit of the vine,

till uncounted millions, heroes and saints,
vindicate scriptures of every faith,

and shatter to pieces the staff of Nimrod
in vanishing worlds of imagined gods.

For Love

> To my grandmother, Marie E. Elliott (1898-1987)

From Time's peril, I return to look,
and seize fragments of memory's favorite
forms. I recall the unpublished

and published works of your heart, the family
you loved and left, but never left loving.
But shed no tears, for separations always

temporal are borne like cresting waves
to shore spilling   spilling   spilling all there,
and I shall swim to you, grandmother,

with a force stronger than the one which brought
me from my mother's womb and she from yours.
Yes, when it is time   when it is time, we

shall bare our spirits again in friendship,
in love, and speak of the long silence
as a memory.

Satori

When we were made joyful by growing things,
    by lands boundless as an evening breeze, where
earth's waters ran, when "eyes of people
    in the East were captivated by arts
and wonders of the West," when eyes of people
    in the West were captivated by love,
in wonder of the East, when mighty winds
    swept over the waters, waters gathered
into one, when dry good land appeared, soil
    gave growth, and earth was living earth, when we
were not angry, or grieved, but full—brimful
    growing—Job before and after the trials,
and no one escapes to tell a tale,
    no tales of life wracked, but of breath in lands
not bloodied, sore, but rich—one soil, one soul.

So from the lovers it comes, a knowing
beyond knowing, a momentary truth
one cannot speak who has not seen lovers

gather what's left from plunder of others.
We are blind, but if not darkness, what could
teach us love, to know how we imagine

a voice as we do the sun or moon when
there is none? Everything fragmentary—
and what the lover knows is illusion

not different from all that is memory,
all that is known. And darkness brings but one
illumination: it's not sin to love

or remember each moving toward light or
Nirvana—recalling only a flame.
Imagine ones who cannot imagine,

then this pain is better, better than none.

Home

(Cape Cod)

I.
Light over oceans, moon tides, high rising crests
breaking waves, wild, rhythmic pounding resounding

on jetties where we'd stand tempting insurmountable
    seas.
Sun's slow decline behind high cliffs, beneath ocean's
    placid

cold, ocean's salty sea; sea stilled in the breeze,
and nostrils full, salty, and foam on one's toes,

and one unrelenting crash of surf, vastness, power
    calling
us into depths of the killing, loving sea.

II.
When Gram's garden needed weeding, she'd stand
behind me to the side, pointing out weeds
from planted things: "Tomatoes, need a stick;
over there is squash, and those two rows are
collards and mustard greens; don't step on them,
careful; walk between the rows." Skillfully,
she'd point out life to come and tell me, "Be

patient, be patient—Everything in its
own time." Light rising over oceans, sun
deathless as a smoldering flame, and days,
inviolable days, full enough
for picking. She'd turned, turned the earth, back bent
with pitchfork and hoe, and behind, Granddad,
with garden hose, watering seeds freshly

buried in black soil, knowing soil will yield.
She hungered for growing, days, growing things:
handmaidens, soft breezes, beach trees growing
without blemish, quivering plums, full vines
and the trellis bright with grapes. Blueberries
in a backfield, berries we would pick and
pick, till bushes stripped, until colanders

brimming, till she made cupboards of jelly,
pancakes plump with berry, and fruit of days
on the land, and something more than food given,
mingling with elements yet unborn.
Something borne by a world, where light shall stand
in delight, and beauty is not forgotten
shadows of earth, the fertile muck in all

beginnings, or passion buried, un-grown.
Be patient, everything has its time,
blossoming, place. And in a land where some
have forsaken the beautiful eyes
and naked strength in salmon, herring
moving upstream, while some have forgotten
celestial glowing, or stars and branches

flowing with bloom, one Placeless Place, before
sadness hung over all houses, compassion,
stretched out—alone, on her bed, recalling
only sweet scent of nature, timorous
love and gilded snows covering the land
in their season there, there—a springtime.
When seed takes hold in darkness of soil, grows

and grows from small life, the stuff spun from silk,
like scented cloth, not sacks of withered grain.

We live in this Age, when the human race,
whole nations in our time grew up singing
songs of war, flashing swords, double-barreled
kingdoms, and teaching tales of Hector, songs
of Achilles, till Orpheus is silent,
Apollo new-fashioned, and Helen's bloom,
a flower faded; Eurydice, lost
in the din, for Time has mellowed neither

horns nor whistles. Even Odysseus,
Mastermind of War, even he tired
of battle, fighting fruitless struggle
full grown. Even he longed to walk among
orchard groves and dance to the Muse, a song
beaten from heart's ghosts. Earth weeps now for lands
overgrown, poetry confined to towers, words,
clamor, voices, echo, a desert wolf.

III.
Moses, He Who conversed with God, a Man
Who had a stammering tongue, trials, spent
years, wilderness years, searching for Canaan;

and He, Jesus, Love's Spirit, spent forty
days, desert days, eating wild berries, wind
and He, Jesus, wept; even forty years

of Baha'u'llah, *The Blessed Beauty,*
locked in Akka's prison, felt grief's full tune,
grief of hearts thirsty from dry deserts,

from desolated places where grass no
longer grows, and what grows is no longer
grass, where God is travel songs, tombstones,

remembered adornment, false tunes, hearth yarns.

IV.
Exhausted, I haul my cargo to caves
for safe keeping, hoping mists rise soon,
to recognize homelands, once more, leaving
heroes, Titans, and Fates of the age
to the wind. And I wish to be remembered,
remembered as one with a song on my
tongue, and mine, a name beyond heart's weeping,
suffering. And flying into Love's arms
more than a girl with lyrics on her tongue, lips,
poetry and pain, eyes longing
for Divine, a world of letters, I wish
to *become*, whole voiced—music and words,
letters of books unopened—wish to say
I was not forsaken in shadow's light,
a broken mirror, life severed from sound
in a world drunk with wine and war, folly,
and age-worn beauty recounted as white-armed
maidens floating across waters like ghosts
or clouds. Oh say, *say* I was swept into
beauty's flameless flames, pressed by sweet embrace,
speaking "Behold, here am I," before swept—

hurled into nothingness, beyond taste, touch
and laughter, I become only the dream you
have dreamt. Wish for swimming past tears, ocean
crests, and ways where I failed to make even one
song. Find me in gales, among nightingales,
hills, winding roads, streams, flowers, find me
in light rising over oceans singing
deathless sun's smoldering flame, among days,
inviolable days, full enough for picking.

ENDNOTES

Configurations
This invocation echoes the beginning of the *Iliad:*
Aeidei di 'Emou: Sings through me
Aeidei dia Sou: Sings through you (from Greek)

In March 1968, the young American Lieutenant, William Calley, was ordered to lead an offensive on the Vietnamese village of Son My (My Lai), which resulted in the death of most village inhabitants and all animals. Pham Thic Trin is one of the few survivors of the My Lai massacre. In 1988, twenty years later, she lived in the family house and tended the single stone monument that commemorated her village.

"Nightmare" in several languages: *Ephialtes* (Greek); *Niht maere* (German); *Pesadilla* (Spanish); *Cauchmar* (French); *Cơn ác mông* (Vietnamese).

Babylon to Baghdad
Babylon: a large metropolis known first for its luxury, and later, its wickedness.

Baghdad: now the capital of Iraq, was near the site of the biblical city of Babylon.

Marduk: a god from Mesopotamian culture and patron deity of the city of Bablyon. Marduk, who created earth and man from his own blood, was a symbol of faith in Babylon, for both the city and the people.

Baha'u'llah: The Prophet-Founder of the Baha'i Faith. *Baha'u'llah,* went to Baghdad when He was exiled from Persia in 1853, and except for the period between 1854 and 1856, He lived in Baghdad and there revealed several sacred tablets and books.

Jewel of the Caribbean

Section I: from *The Book of Job* (2: 11-13).

Section II-VII: the names Macandal to Aristide are those of Haiti's Presidents in chronological order. References taken from *Written in Blood: The Story of the Haitian People, 1492-1995*, Michael Heinl (University Press of America, Inc.: Lanham, MD, 1996; pp. 788-799).

Section II-III,V, VIII: Many historical references taken from *Written in Blood: The Story of the Haitian People, 1492-1995*, Michael Heinl (University Press of America, Inc.; Lanham, MD, 1996). This is a revised and expanded edition of text originally by Robert and Nancy Heinl (Houghton Mifflin Co.: Boston, MA, 1966).

—Taino Indians: Haiti's original natives: Michael Heinl (p. 11).
—Information regarding U.S. aid sent to Haiti, 1959-1968: Michael Heinl (pp. 587-93)
—quotations of President Francois Duvalier, Michael Heinl (pp. 575-76, 607, 623).
— quotations of U.S. Presidents on Haitian leadership: Michael Heinl (pp. 571, 608).
—Tonton Macoutes: Francois Duvalier's Paramilitary police, feared by the people for their brutality, intimidation and acts of terror: Michael Heinl (p. 628).
—18th century French saying describing colonial wealth: *Rich as a Creole:* Michael Heinl (p. 31).
—Words of 1800's planter: *The security of the whites... ignorance:* Michael Heinl (p. 25).
—Words of Moreau de Saint-Mery: Michael Heinl (p. 30).
—Code Noir: Michael Heinl (pp. 24-26).
—*Make their feet leave the earth:* Under Francois Duvalier's regime, the saying that meant "death" by Tonton Macoutes was "Make his feet leave the earth." Michael Heinl (p. 632).
—Selected history of Francois Duvalier's 14 year regime: Michael Heinl (pp. 561-627).
—1492-1697, chronology of Haitian colonial rule: Michael Heinl (p. 788).

—1994 U.S. sends 20,000 troops to Haiti deposing Haitian military and reinstating Jean Bertrand-Aristide in a rousing welcome as Haiti's democratically elected President *(Encarta.msn/Aristide, Jean-Bertrand).*

Section VII: Sermon excerpts of Aristide: *In the Parish of the Poor, Writings from Haiti,* by Jean Bertrand-Aristide, (Orbis Books: 1990), pp. 74 and 23, respectively.

In T-claude, etc. the T is a shortened form of *petite,* which means little or small in French.

Section X: ARISTIDE FLIES INTO EXILE: Headline, *The Washington Post,* March 1, 2004.
—I WAS FORCED TO RESIGN… GUNPOINT: *CNN* news crawl, March 2004.
—WASHINGTON DECLARES… SECOND THOUGHTS: *CNN* news crawl, March 2004.

Boat People: a term first used to describe Indochinese refugees fleeing communist rule after the Vietnam War (1975) in small boats, and millions of people who left Vietnam after China's invasion of Vietnam in 1979. More than one million boat people perished at sea and others, upon reaching Southeast Asian countries, learned they could not remain permanently. The U.S., Canada, and other nations accepted most of the refugees in the late 1970's and 1980's. The boat people were described as political and economic refugees.

Haitian Boat People: A term applied also to political and economic refugees who fled their homeland by similar means—small boats. All references from various news headlines, (Immigrationlinks.com); this site provides many news articles about plight of Haitian boat people.

Conflicting news headlines reporting Aristide's reasons for flight from Haiti, March 1, 2004: All references taken from various headlines.

Crepusculo
Crespusculo: Spanish word for "twilight."

Italics: multiple explosions in Karbala, from *CNN* news broadcast.

Karbala/Karbila—a city in Iraq, also the Shrine city of the Imam Husayn and the site of His martyrdom. Imam Husayn: The third Imam, in Shi'ih Islam, grandson of the Prophet Muhammad.

Mengele
Josef Mengele, known as The Angel of Death, was the Nazi doctor of Auschwitz concentration camp (1943-45). He carried out gruesome medical experiments and selected hundreds of thousands of Jews for gassing in crematoriums. Having eluded capture by allied forces in 1945, Mengele is believed to have moved to Brazil, and was reported to have drowned in 1986 in Sao Paulo, Brazil.

Bungalow 5555 Alvenega Road: believed to be Josef Mengele's last address.

Pangaea
The theory of continental drift posits that the earth's crust is divided into contiguous moving plates and carries embedded continents. Contemporary geologists theorize that 200 million years ago, there existed a supercontinent, Pangaea, whose movement of splitting and resplitting resulted in today's continents and islands.

The Man From Virginia
In 1998, Spectrum Gallery in Washington, D.C. sponsored an Art and Poetry show. In preparation for the exhibit, in 1997, the gallery invited several poets in the greater Washington area to visit them and select three or four artists whose work, stylistically, inspired a poetic response; although the artist and poet pairing was narrowed by this process, the gallery selected the final pairs, limiting the pairing to one of the writer's choices.

Sculptor Carol Gellner Levin, the artist with whom I was
    partnered and am gratefully indebted to, inspired the
    poem, which takes its title from her sculpture entitled,
    The Man From Virginia.

All quotations in parts I, II, III, V, and X are taken from real
    events and news stories.

Odysseus in the Underworld

The fragments, *You must long for daylight. Go quickly. Sinews
    no longer bind* and *My Shining Odysseus* from *The
    Odyssey* by Homer, translated by Robert Fagles, copyright
    (c) 1996 by Robert Fagles. Published by Viking Penguin, a
    division of Penguin Group (USA) Inc. (256).

Toward the Silence

Written in memory of my teacher and distinguished poet,
    Robert Hayden. Consultant to The Library of Congress
    1978-1980, Hayden also taught contemporary poetry at
    Howard University from 1978 to 1980.

A Sacred Geometry

Geometria: linking together numbers and letters, a system
    used particularly in the relationship to the Names of God
    and their number equivalents; from Latin, the branch of
    mathematics that deals with measurement, properties,
    and relationships of points, lines, angles, surfaces, and
    solids; a particular system of geometry.

Ancient Greeks believed prime numbers constituted the
    language of the Divine, and Plato thought geometry was
    an ideal philosophical language. To Plato, Pythagoras,
    and Nicomachus, mathematics was a universal language
    indicative of the Creator's Mind, and the idea of number
    mysticism was passed on from the ancient world to the
    Medieval world permeating Judaism, Christianity, Islam
    and similar systems in India and China. In the Christian
    world, St. Augustine wrote about numbers and geometric
    forms as a method for contemplating the language of the
    heavens, and the number nine–the triplication of three—
    became symbol of the Holy Spirit. In *The Divine Comedy,*

Dante used the number nine to describe the circles of hell, Purgatory, and the heavens of Paradise. The number nine is significant also in the Baha'i Faith, where it is a symbol for the Name of God in this Day and of human unity.

Baha: a word meaning Glory; also in the Baha'i Faith, *Baha* means The Greatest Name, and is a title by which Baha'u'llah is designated. *Baha* is also the first month of the Baha'i year: from sunset 20 March to sunset 8 April.

Quadrivium: a group of studies consisting of arithmetic, music, geometry, and astronomy and forming the courses for three years of study between B.A. and M.A. degrees in a medieval university.

Geomancy: divination by means of figures or lines.

The poem "A Sacred Geometry" was inspired by conversations with my dear friend, Professor Julie Badiee, who died much too young on May 20, 2001. Dr. Badiee, who received her PhD from University of Michigan in Islamic Art, was a full Professor of Art History for 22 years at McDaniel College, formerly Western Maryland College. Her book, *An Earthly Paradise*, reveals how gardens, circles, and geometric forms have been used as metaphors for the spiritual life in the sacred spaces of the world's major religions.

Worlds From Babel, Two Towers, 9/11

Tower of Babel: The significance lies in the ancient story explaining the origin of diverse languages of humankind. In the tale, humans attempted to build a tower to heaven and make a name for themselves; the builders were struck down by God for their prideful action, and the Lord made a babble of their language and scattered humans all over the face of earth.

—Tower: the center of the Mesopotamian city consisting of a complex of buildings and a temple pyramid extending upwards to a "gate" in the heavens through which gods came down and revealed themselves.

—Babel: a term for the Babylonians which meant, the *gate of the gods.*

Florence

The words in italics at poem's end are taken from *Italian Literature,* Vol. I, John Addington Symonds (p. 50).

Dying for Religion

Nimrod: Old Testament king, a mighty hunter and great-grandson to Noah. Nimrod's kingdom consisted of Babel, Erech, and Accad, all in the land of Shinar.

Satori

Satori: the state of intuitive illumination sought in Zen Buddhism.

Words in italics are taken from *The Tablets of Baha'u'llah.* The entire line from *Tablets* reads, "When the eyes of the people in the East were captivated by the arts and wonders of the West." (p. 144).

Home

Baha'u'llah: Prophet-Founder of the Baha'i Faith

The Blessed Beauty: a title sometimes applied to *Baha'u'llah* by Baha'is.

Akka: Arabic name for the port city of Akko (known in ancient times as Accho, in the late classical period as Ptolemais, and in the crusader era as St Jean d' Acre), located on the coast of what is now Israel, near Haifa. In the nineteenth century, Akka was a prison-city or penal colony of the Turkish empire; the city was a place so foul that it was said a bird flying over Akka would drop dead from the stench. In 1868, Baha'u'llah was banished to Akka, and on His arrival, He named it the Most Great Prison. He and his family were imprisoned in the prison barracks from 1868-1870.

ABOUT THE AUTHOR

DONNA DENIZÉ, of Haitian-American descent, is the author of the poetry chapbook, *The Lover's Voice*. Her poems have appeared in several anthologies including, *Whose Woods These Are; Hungry As We Are; WPFW Poetry Anthology; Ribbon of Song; Natives, Tourists, and Other Mysteries; Weavings 2000*, and such magazines as *Provincetown Arts, Gargoyle*, and *World Order*.

She holds degrees from Stonehill College and Howard University, and received grants from The Johns Hopkins University Summer Writing Program; Duke University Writer's Conference; the Bread Loaf School of English, Lincoln College at Oxford University; the D.C. Humanities Council, and The Folger Shakespeare Library's Teaching Shakespeare Institute. She served two years on The Folger Poetry Board, and was a contributor to *Shakespeare Set Free,* a three volume set on teaching Shakespeare, published by The Folger.

She has been the recipient of distinguished teacher awards at St. Albans, the White House Commission on Presidential Scholars, and Williams College, which awarded her the George Olmsted Jr., Prize for excellence in secondary teaching. She currently teaches literature at St. Albans School for Boys in Washington, D.C., and her educational philosophy is based on Baha'i principles.

Ms. Denizé was the Invited Teacher/Participant in The Corporation for Public Broadcasting's eight-part mini-series, *In Search of the Novel* (aired nationwide, 2000-present) and has served through appointment by Governor Charles Robb to The Virginia State Advisory Board on Vocational Education.

ABOUT THE ARTIST

THEO MOORE is an artist and musician from Cape Cod, MA. He holds a BFA from the University of Massachusetts at Amherst and recently spent a year at the American Academy in Rome as a Visiting Artist. He currently lives in New York City with his wife, Molly, and son, Mason.

ABOUT THE CAPITAL COLLECTION

The CAPITAL COLLECTION is an imprint by The Word Works that features excellence in poetry from authors in the Greater Washington, DC area. The hallmark of this series is that each book selected is financially supported by advance book sales and community contributions. The author also agrees to work with the press to promote the Capital Collection books, support other activities of The Word Works, and increase public interest in poetry.

The following individuals and organizations have contributed to the Capital Collection to make this book possible:

PATRONS:
    Robert and Nancy Carr
    Ikemba Iweala
    Mark and Kimberly Johnson
    Lou Stovall

DONORS:
    Karren L. Alenier
    Marta Dunetz
    Miles David Moore
    Lucille Stuberville
    Angela and Courtney Vance

FRIENDS:
    Paul and Celeste Bergan
    Daniel Healy
    Mark and Martha Jane Mullin
    Jane Porter
    Ruth and Bill Selig
    Rosemary Walsh
    Z. Vance Wilson

ABOUT THE WORD WORKS

THE WORD WORKS, a nonprofit literary organization, publishes contemporary poetry in collectors' editions. Since 1981, the organization has sponsored the Washington Prize, a $1,500 award to an American poet. Monthly, The Word Works presents free literary programs in the Chevy Chase Café Muse series, and each summer, free poetry programs are held at the historic Joaquin Miller Cabin in Washington, DC's Rock Creek Park. Annually, two high school students debut in the Miller Cabin Series as winners of the Young Poets Competition.

Since 1974, Word Works programs have included: "In the Shadow of the Capitol," a symposium and archival project on the African-American intellectual community in segregated Washington, DC; the Gunston Arts Center Poetry Series (Ai, Carolyn Forché, Stanley Kunitz, and others); the Poet-Editor panel discussions at the Bethesda Writer's Center (John Hollander, Maurice English, Anthony Hecht, Josephine Jacobsen, and others); Poet's Jam, a multi-arts program series featuring poetry in performance; a poetry workshop at the Center for Creative Non-Violence (CCNV) shelter; and the Arts Retreat in Tuscany. Master Class workshops, an ongoing program, have featured Agha Shahid Ali, Thomas Lux, and Marilyn Nelson.

In 2005, Word Works will have published 57 titles, including work from such authors as Deirdra Baldwin, J.H. Beall, Christopher Bursk, John Pauker, Edward Weismiller, and Mac Wellman. Currently, The Word Works publishes books and occasional anthologies under three imprints: the Washington Prize, the Capital Collection, and International Editions.

Past grants have been awarded by the National Endowment for the Arts, National Endowment for the Humanities, DC Commission on the Arts & Humanities, Witter Bynner Foundation, Writer's Center, Bell Atlantic, Batir Foundation, and others, including many generous private patrons.

THE WORD WORKS has established an archive of artistic and administrative materials in the Washington Writing Archive housed in the George Washington University Gelman Library.

Please enclose a self-addressed, stamped envelope with all inquiries.

THE WORD WORKS   PO Box 42164 Washington, DC 20015
editor@wordworksdc.com   www.wordworksdc.com

WORD WORKS BOOKS

Karren L. Alenier, *Wandering on the Outside*
Karren L. Alenier, Hilary Tham, Miles David Moore, eds.,
  Winners: A Retrospective of the Washington Prize
* Nathalie F. Anderson, *Following Fred Astaire*
* Michael Atkinson, *One Hundred Children Waiting for a Train*
Mel Belin, *Flesh That Was Chrysalis* (CAPITAL COLLECTION)
* Peter Blair, *Last Heat*
* Carrie Bennett, *biography of water*
Doris Brody, *Judging the Distance* (CAPITAL COLLECTION)
Grace Cavalieri, *Pinecrest Rest Haven* (CAPITAL COLLECTION)
Christopher Conlon, *Gilbert and Garbo in Love*
  (CAPITAL COLLECTION)
Moshe Dor, Barbara Goldberg, Giora Leshem, eds.,
  The Stones Remember
* Linda Lee Harper, *Toward Desire*
James Hopkins, *Eight Pale Women* (CAPITAL COLLECTION)
* Ann Rae Jonas, *A Diamond Is Hard But Not Tough*
Myong-Hee Kim, *Crow's Eye View: The Infamy of Lee Sang,
  Korean Poet* (INTERNATIONAL EDITIONS)
Vladimir Levchev, *Black Book of the Endangered Species*
  (INTERNATIONAL EDITIONS)
* Fred Marchant, *Tipping Point*
Judith McCombs, *The Habit of Fire* (CAPITAL COLLECTION)
* Ron Mohring, *Survivable World*
Miles David Moore, *The Bears of Paris* (CAPITAL COLLECTION)
Miles David Moore, *Rollercoaster* (CAPITAL COLLECTION)
Jacklyn Potter, Dwaine Rieves, Gary Stein, eds.
  Cabin Fever: Poets at Joaquin Miller's Cabin
* Jay Rogoff, *The Cutoff*
Robert Sargent, *Aspects of a Southern Story*
Robert Sargent, *A Woman From Memphis*
* Enid Shomer, *Stalking the Florida Panther*
Maria Terrone, *The Bodies We Were Loaned* (CAPITAL COLLECTION)
Hilary Tham, *Bad Names for Women* (CAPITAL COLLECTION)
Hilary Tham, *Counting* (CAPITAL COLLECTION)
Jonathan Vaile *Blue Cowboy* (CAPITAL COLLECTION)
* Miles Waggener, *Phoenix Suites*
* Charlotte Gould Warren, *Gandhi's Lap*
* George Young, *Spinoza's Mouse*

  * Washington Prize winners